HAIR
Do It Yourself!

Dress your hair up

with some fun styles...

E.L. Johnson

HAIR
DO IT YOURSELF!

Copyright © 2012 by E.L. Johnson

All rights reserved. No part of this publication may be reproduced, stored in a retrieval system, or transmitted in any form or by any means—electronic, mechanical, photocopying, recording, or any other—except for brief quotations in printed reviews, without prior permission of the copyright owner or publisher. Any unauthorized publication is an infringement of the copyright law.

ISBN-13: 978-1-926676-71-5

Published by Word Alive Press
131 Cordite Road, Winnipeg, MB R3W 1S1
www.wordalivepress.ca

Printed in Canada.

Library and Archives Canada Cataloguing in Publication

Johnson, E.L., 1968-
      Hair : do it yourself! / E.L. Johnson.

ISBN 978-1-77069-378-4

      1. Hairstyles--Juvenile literature. 2. Ornamental hairwork--Juvenile literature. 3. Hairdressing--Juvenile literature. 4. Hair--Care and hygiene--Juvenile literature. I. Title.

TT972.J64 2011   j646.7'24   C2011-906312-3

This book is dedicated to
My three Es, with lots of love.

Author's Note

Thank you for your interest in Hair, Do it yourself!

Hair has been a fascination with me since the age of 10. My background evolves mainly in the areas of arts, hairdo's, textiles and designs. It was when I became a licensed hairstylist that I found my passion in creating a variety of different styles of hairdo's. Later to be used for special occasions, such as weddings, birthday parties,etc. Hair can be in different variations; it can be cut, permed, straightened, coloured, curled, styled and even extended. Hair can also make a statement or be a trademark of a person.

This book is for all those who want to be creative and different when it comes to wacky hair days, school spirit days, sport team game days, parties and custom-made hair costumes for the odd occasions.

My inspiration are my children.

Thank you to all who helped and participated in its creation.

Enjoy and have fun!

Table of Contents

What is hair? 1
Anatomy of the head 3
Hairs what you will need—supplies 4
Hair Techniques 5
Angel 7
Butterfly 8
Cat 9
Christmas tree 10
Crown 11
Deer 12
Double happiness 13
Flower 14
Football 15
Go Team 16
Hat 17
Horse 18
Indian girl 19
Mouse ears 20
Nest 21
Octopus 22
Panda bear 23
Rabbit 24
Soccer 25
Spider 26
Sun 27
Tree 28
Notes 29
Letters of the alphabet 29

What is hair?

Hair is art...

You can decorate it and make all kinds of shapes and sizes.

Hair keeps our heads warm.

Hair is for adornment.

Hair is a statement.

Hair can be a signature of a person. Think of Elvis, Justin Bieber, Hannah Montana, Princess Leah, etc. We recognize them by the style of their hair.

Hair is dressed up for special occasions, proms and weddings.

Hair grows half an inch every month and can be cut to a style to create a different look.

Hair is straight, curly, and wavy.

Hair is thin, thick, short and long.

Hair can be coloured—black, brown, red, yellow and sometimes ... blue!

Hair turns grey/white naturally at a certain age or depends on our generations.

Hair loss is normal. We lose about 50-150 hairs per day, and it grows back.

Hair can be permed, twisted, braided, wrapped around, crimped, curled, straightened, teased, spiked, beaded and extended.

Hair (up to 10 inches) can be donated for a great cause in making wigs and putting a smile on someone.

Hair can change a way a person feels and changes the look of a person.

Sometimes we may have a BHD (Bad Hair Day), but with a new haircut or style, we feel great once again!

Hair is an extension to your personality!

Anatomy of the head

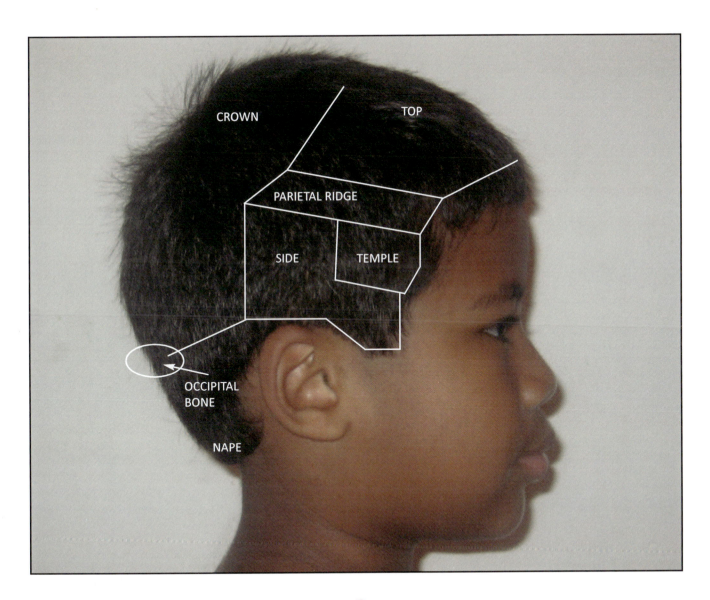

Supply List

1. Gel and hairspray
2. Elastics—small for the hair ends and thick for making ponytails
3. Pipe cleaners in assorted colours
4. Felt
5. Coffee sticks and popsicle sticks (painted or use marker to desired colour)
6. Hair pins
7. Hair pins with beads for decoration
8. Bobby pins
9. Washable make-up (and other supplies to decorate) can be purchased at local dollar store or party store
10. Brush and tail comb
11. Washable hair colour spray

Hair Techniques

Bend pipe cleaners into the elastics.
(Fine hair—2 pipe cleaners,
Thick hair—3 pipe cleaners)

Begin braiding with 3 strands with
the pipe cleaner and crisscross over
into the middle until you reach the end.

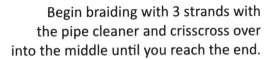

Wrap hair ends around the pipe cleaner
and bending it to hold in place. Finish with
an elastic at end of braid to hold in excess hair.

Stand up braid: use a popsicle stick and slide it
through the braid, into the elastic to secure it.
Make sure you double-elastic for extra support.
Use black marker (or depending on your hair
colour) to colour in stick and cut off remainder.

Wrap hair around the pipe cleaner
and use an elastic on the end.
Shape to desired look.

Please refer to these diagrams when creating the hairstyles.

Angel

Hair Length: Medium

Supplies: 2 pink pipe cleaners (for fine hair), 3 elastics, 1 pink popsicle stick, accessorize with boa and bow with beads

Estimated Time: 30 minutes

How To:

* Make 1 ponytail using 2 thick elastics at the top of the crown.

* Place 2 pipe cleaners into elastic and start braiding. About 2 inches up from braid, stop and use an elastic.

* Divide hair into 2 braids and connect the ends to each other with pipe cleaners, forming a circle.

* Use popsicle stick the same height of braid and insert it into the elastic for secure hold.

* Use pink boa and twist it around the halo and tie ribbon on the back and beads to decorate end of ribbon.

Butterfly

Hair Length: Medium to Long

Supplies: 12 pipe cleaners, 9 coloured elastics, hairpins, beads (through the hair pins to accessorize, and 2 little pom-poms (for antennas), washable haircolour

Estimated Time: 45 minutes

How To:

Section hair into 5 parts, leaving a section down in the middle. Start ponytail at each side on the top of forehead, closest to the antennas. Bend 3 pipe cleaners into the elastic and start braiding. Use elastic with pipe cleaner to wrap around the ends. Make a ponytail at the bottom part of crown. Repeat with 3 pipe cleaners and start braiding. You can pick any colour you want for your butterfly. Start your braid at the nape and work your way to the forehead. Put elastic on and tuck end of braid in with hair pins. With a black pipe cleaner, pull it through the braid and bend it, then add the pom-poms. To form the shape of the butterfly, connect the end of the top braid to the bottom top braid with the leftover pipe cleaners. Tuck the bottom end braid with hair pins to the bottom of the body part.

Decorate your butterfly with beads and washable hair colour.

Cat

Hair Length: Medium

Supplies: 4 pipe cleaners (2 for each braid), 4 elastics and bobby pins, face make-up

Estimated Time: 30 minutes

How To:

* Section hair down the middle and make 2 ponytails at the top of the crown.

* Use 2 pipe cleaners for each braid and tuck them into the elastics.

* Once braids are completed, secure ends with elastic or wrap pipe cleaner around the ends and bend braid in the middle.

* Tuck the ends inwards towards the head and secure with bobby pins.

* Use washable face paint for nose and whiskers.

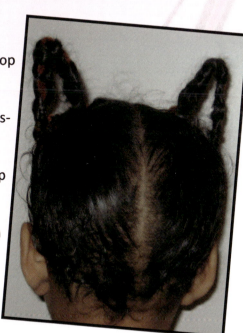

Christmas Tree

Hair Length: Long

Supplies: 8 Black pipe cleaners, elastics, hair pins, decorations for tree

Estimated Time: 45 minutes

How To:

* Make a ponytail at the top of crown.

* Use 7 pipe cleaners and bend them into the elastic.

* Section hair into 7 strands and wrap hair around each pipe cleaner, leaving 1 pipe cleaner in centre for support.

* Secure with elastics at the end.

* Bend each strand into the shape of a tree and connect them to the centre pipe cleaner.

* Once they're all connected, add a star on top of the tree and decorate it with presents and balls.

Crown

Hair Length: Long

Supplies: 6 yellow pipe cleaners, elastics, hair pins, bobby pins and beads for decorations

Estimated Time: 45 minutes

How To:

* Section hair into 6 ponytails: 4 sections on top of head and 2 sections at the back of head.

* Section the hair from ear to ear on the top of the crown. Make 2 braids, starting at the back of the head, and join the ends at the front with a pipe cleaner.

* Make 4 braids at the top of the head to the crown. Start the braids beside each other above the ears. The 2 front braids join at the front with pipe cleaner and back braids connect the ends to the back of the ponytail elastics.

* Use bobby pins to secure in place and add beads into hair pins and decorate.

Deer

Hair Length: Medium to long

Supplies: 10 brown pipe cleaners, elastics, bobby pins, 2 popsicle sticks

Estimated Time: 45 minutes

How To:

* Section hair into 4 ponytails: Down the middle and from ear to ear.

* Make 2 ponytails at top of the head for ears and use 2 pipe cleaners for each. Make 2 ponytails at the crown for antlers and use 3 pipe cleaners for each.

* Start braiding and then bend the ears in shape, tucking the ends inward and use bobby pins to hold.

* Braid the antlers half way and put elastic on. Separate the strands and twist hair around the pipe cleaner, leaving the middle one to finish braid.

* Finish off with the stick for a secure hold by sliding it in from the back.

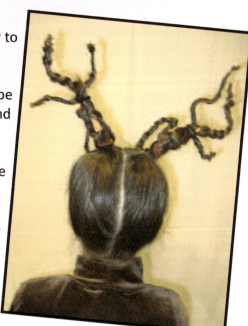

Double Happiness

Hair Length: Medium to long

Supplies: 8 pipe cleaners, elastics and bobby pin

Estimated Time: 45 minutes–1 hour

How To:

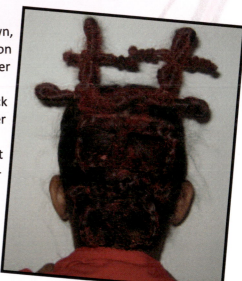

* Section hair down the middle from the top of the head to the crown, making 2 ponytails. The back part of the crown to nape area, section hair horizontally making 3 ponytails (Second ponytail make smaller section).
* Start at the nape area, dividing ponytail into 2 braids with 1 black pipe cleaner for each. Wrap hair ends with remaining pipe cleaner and bend into 2 squares connecting it with bobby pins.
* Second ponytail, divide into 2, add 2 black pipe cleaners and twist each section of hair around the pipe cleaner. Bend them in the middle with the ends crossing.
* Third ponytail, dividing ponytail into 2 braids with 1 black pipe cleaner for each. Wrap hair ends with remaining pipe cleaner and bend into 2 squares connecting it with bobby pins.
* The last 2 ponytails on top of the crown, divide each into 3 even strands with 3 pipe cleaners and twist each section of hair around the pipe cleaner. Stand up and bend the middle strand and use elastic to secure the bottom. The other 2 strands, bend them and use elastic to secure each side at the bottom and bend each strand to form a t and use elastics.

Flower

Hair Length: Medium to Long

Supplies: 12 pink pipe cleaners, elastics, bobby pins, accessorize with butterfly, washable hair colour

Estimated Time: 45 minutes

How To:

* Section hair into 6 ponytails and begin at one side on top of the crown and make your first ponytail.

* When one braid ends, bend and attach to the beginning of another braid with pipe cleaner.

* When braids are completed, attach a butterfly and spray flower with washable hair colour. (Optional: wear green to look like the stem)

Football

Hair Length: Short

Supplies: Gel, hairspray, green hair colour spray, football and goal post (from your local dollar store or party supply store), clip, glue or needle and thread to hold football to clip

Estimated Time: 45 minutes

How To:

* Use gel and hairspray on the top of the head and wait half an hour for hair to dry and harden.

* Cover face with a towel and spray washable green hairspray on top of head.

* Wait 5 minutes, then secure goal post with silver hair clip and glue or needle and thread silver clip to hold football and clip football to hair.

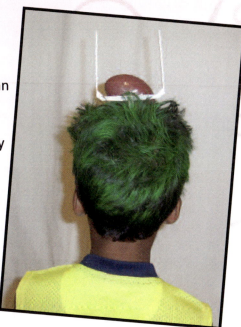

Go Team

Hair Length: Shoulder length

Supplies: 12 pipe cleaners, elastics, hair pins, bobby pins

Estimated Time: 1 hour

How To:

* Section hair evenly from top of head to nape into 7 ponytails.

* Make ponytails on top of crown from ear to ear and leave some space between words

* Tuck pipe cleaners into elastic and braid.

* Optional, to secure letters in stand up position, place hair pin at the back of the letters into the elastic.

G - One ponytail, two braids (1 long braid with pipe cleaner on top and 1 short braid with pipe cleaner on bottom). Shape into the letter G.

O - One ponytail, one braid, one pipe cleaner and wrap hair ends with elastic and with remaining pipe cleaner, wrap around and connect to ponytail. Shape into letter O.

T - One ponytail, two pipe cleaners, braid half way up and put elastic on and make two braids for the top of letter T. If ends are too long, bend them to shape and secure with elastic. Shape into letter T.

E - One ponytail, two braids (1 long braid with pipe cleaner on top and 1 short braid with pipe cleaner on bottom). Cut a small piece of pipe cleaner and add it in the middle. Shape into the letter E.

A - One ponytail, one braid, one pipe cleaner. Once braid is complete, bend braid in half and secure end with elastic and remaining pipe cleaner wrap around onto next ponytail. Shape into letter A.

M - Two ponytails, two braids and one pipe cleaner for each braid. Bend braids and join the ends with elastic and remaining pipe cleaner. (cut off pipe cleaner if too long). Shape into letter M.

Hat with extensions

Hair Length: Shoulder length

Supplies: 4 strands of hair, braided (local dollar store), loufah with hole in the middle, bobby pins, pipe cleaner, flower, elastic, thread and needle

Estimated Time: 1 hour

How To:

* Go to your local dollar store and purchase 4 strands of black hair (or desired colour).
  You may have to braid them and attach 2 braids together side by side with needle and thread. Join one end together to form a circle and leave the other end later to adjust the size when placing on the head.
* Make a ponytail at the top of crown and place circular loufah through the ponytail.
* Back comb the hair underneath and spread it all around the loufah, tucking the ends underneath with bobby pins.
* Place braids on the head and adjust to size and sew up the ends together. The braids are used as the brim (edge) of a hat. Use bobby pins to secure in place.
* Accessorize with a flower on the side.

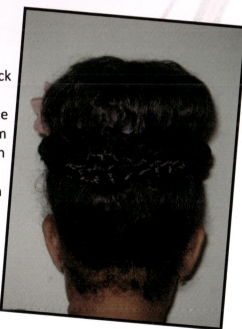

Horse

Hair Length: Shoulder length

Supplies: 6 pipe cleaners, elastics and bobby pins

Estimated Time: 30 minutes

How To:

* Section hair into 3 parts, leaving the middle, and make 2 ponytails at the side of the crown.

* Use 3 pipe cleaners for each braid and then bend them in the middle, pinning the ends inward using bobby pins to secure.

* Leave the middle for the mane.

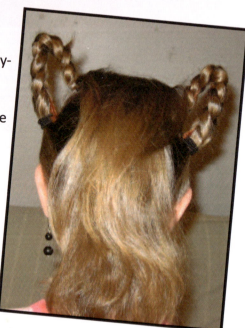

Indian Girl

Hair Length: Shoulder length

Supplies: Elastics, bobby pins, feather

Estimated Time: 40 minutes

How To:

* Section hair down the middle and make 4 ponytails. (2 at top back of crown and 2 at the sides)

* Take a small circular section on top back of crown and make 2 braids then join the ends at the front of forehead with pipe cleaner.

* Use bobby pins to secure in place.

* Make 2 ponytails at the side and braid.

* Add feather at the back with bobby pin to secure.

Mouse Ears

Hair Length: Shoulder length

Supplies: 4 black pipe cleaners, 2 elastics, bobby pins, hair pins, black felt, big red bow, hair clip for bow, black washable make-up for face, costume—white gloves and outfit, thread and needle

Estimated Time: 30 minutes

How To:

* Section hair down the middle and make 2 ponytails at the top of the crown.

* Use 2 pipe cleaners for each braid and wrap the ends with pipe cleaner.

* Bend the ends inward on the side of the head and secure with bobby pins.

* Cut out black felt in the shape of ears and attach with hair pins or needle and black thread.

* Use washable face paint to paint eyes and nose black and attach red bow with silver hair clip to top of head.

Nest

Hair Length: Long hair

Supplies: Elastics, bobby pins, hair pins, tape or glue eggs on the silver clips and bird (optional)

Estimated Time: 45 minutes

How To:

* Section hair evenly into 8 ponytails.

* Make ponytails at the top of the crown to form a circle.

* Braid the 8 ponytails and arrange them to form a nest.

* Pin the braids in a circle and piling them on top of each other using bobby pins to secure.

* Accessorize with eggs and bird (optional) (glue gun silver clip to eggs).

Octopus

Hair Length: Shoulder length

Supplies: 8 pipe cleaners, elastics, bobby pins, styrofoam cup and eyes

Estimated Time: 45 minutes

How To:

* Make a circle at top of head and place a ponytail in centre of crown.

* Section bottom part into 8 ponytails using 1 or 2 pipe cleaners for each braid (1 for thin hair and 2 for thick hair) and wrap ends with elastic.

* Cut out the bottom of a styrofoam cup and place on the ponytail, pulling hair out through the cup.

* Brush hair back (back combing) so that it covers the cup and tuck the ends underneath the cup and secure with bobby pins.

* With a bobby pin, poke the back of the eyes and attach it to the top of the cup and arrange the arms accordingly.

Panda Bear

Hair Length: Shoulder length

Supplies: 4 black pipe cleaners, 2 elastics, bobby pins, hair pins, black felt, washable make-up for face, thread and needle

Estimated Time: 30 minutes

How To:

* Section hair down the middle and make 2 ponytails at the top of the crown.

* Use 2 pipe cleaners for each braid and wrap the ends with pipe cleaner.

* Bend the ends inward on the side of the head and secure with bobby pins.

* Cut out black felt in the shape of ears and attach with hair pins or needle and black thread.

* Use washable face paint to paint eyes and nose black and face white.

Rabbit

Hair Length: Medium to Long

Supplies: 6 white pipe cleaners, elastics, bobby pins, pink felt cut into triangles and washable make-up for face, thread and needle

Estimated Time: 30 minutes

How To:

* Section hair down the middle making 2 ponytails at top of crown.

* Use 3 pipe cleaners for each braid and wrap hair ends around pipe cleaner by bending it and putting an elastic at end.

* Bend braid in the middle to make bunny ears and tuck end of braid inward with bobby pins.

* Attach pink felt triangles to the ears with hair pins or needle and thread to complete the rabbit look.

Soccer

Hair Length: Short

Supplies: Gel, hairspray, green colour hairspray, magnetic soccer ball (or small soccer ball glued to a clip), net (from your local dollar store or party supply store)

Estimated Time: 45 minutes

How To:

* Use gel and hairspray on the top of the head and wait half a hour for hair to dry and harden.

* Cover face with a towel and spray washable green hairspray on top of head.

* Wait about 5 minutes, then secure net with hair clips and place magnetic soccer ball near the front.

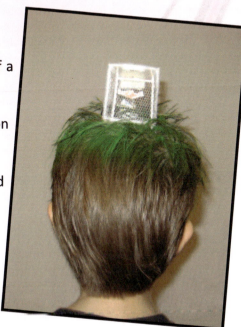

Spider

Hair Length: Medium to Long

Supplies: 12 pipe cleaners, 1 black pipe cleaner for antenna, elastics, and bobby pins

Estimated Time: 45 minutes

How To:

* Divide hair into 8 sections. Start at the top of the head down to the nape area and make 2 sections in the middle.

* Small section at top of head with a ponytail and add black pipe cleaner around elastic for antenna. Backcomb the hair, smooth the top and make a roll by tucking ends inward with bobby pins.

* Bigger section from crown to nape area with ponytail at nape. Backcomb the hair underneath and smooth out top, tucking ends inward with bobby pins.

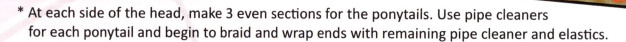

* At each side of the head, make 3 even sections for the ponytails. Use pipe cleaners for each ponytail and begin to braid and wrap ends with remaining pipe cleaner and elastics.

* Bend the braids to look like spider legs and hold secure the base of the ponytail with bobby pins.

Sun

Hair Length: Medium to Long

Supplies: 14 yellow pipe cleaners, 14 elastics, bobby pins

Estimated Time: 30 minutes

How To:

* Section hair from top to bottom into 7 ponytails for the sun rays (or as many rays as you like).

* Make ponytails at the top of your crown and start braiding with 2 yellow pipe cleaners (bend pipe cleaner ends into elastic for secure hold). Don't cut off the ends yet; you will use them to wrap around the ponytails later.

* Once you have braided all your ponytails, start bending them in the middle to make triangles and wrap remaining pipe cleaner to connect them all.

Tree

Hair Length: Medium to Long

Supplies: 18 brown or green pipe cleaners, elastics, leaves to accessorize

Estimated Time: 45 minutes

How To:

* Section hair evenly into 6 parts (or 8-10 depending on how many branches you would like).

* Each braid should have three pipe cleaners.

* Start braiding till you get halfway and use elastics.

* Begin wrapping three hair strands around each pipe cleaner and using elastics to secure the ends.

* When all braids are completed, add your leaves to accessorize by attaching them with pipe cleaners.

Letters of the Alphabet

Notes:
Please read before making your letters and styles.

* Always begin your ponytail with a thick elastic. (no rubber bands, as they will pull your hair or break).

* Make note the amount of pipe cleaner used for thin hair (2) or thick hair (3) and tuck them into the elastics. To get a smooth and clean look, brush your hair towards the ponytail and use hairspray. Brush is used for smoothing and backcombing and tail comb is used for sectioning hair and smoothing.

* When wrapping hair ends with remaining pipe cleaners, you can use small transparent elastics for cleaner ends.

* Hair should be shoulder length or longer to achieve these letters and styles.

* Colour of pipe cleaner and elastics should be used according to hair colour or desired look.

* To make letters stand out, you can use washable hair colour.

* Double up elastic when using popsicle stick.

Now, on to the letters!

A - Section hair down the middle (centre) and make 2 ponytails at each side of top of crown. Use 3 pipe cleaners for each braid. Halfway through one braid, divide a strand and braid it, then connect to other side. Now divide the remaining hair into 3 strands and wrap ends with pipe cleaner and form the letter A. Slide long wooden stick alongside standing braid, for support.

Letters of the Alphabet

B - Make 1 ponytail on your top right side of your crown slightly off centre. Divide hair with 1 short braid with 1 pipe cleaner for bottom letter and 1 long braid with 2 pipe cleaners. Connect the ends with remaining pipe cleaner in the middle. Use bobby pin to secure bottom braid and shape into letter B.

C - Make 1 ponytail on your top right side of your crown slightly off centre. Divide hair with 1 short braid with 1 pipe cleaner for bottom letter and 1 long braid with 2 pipe cleaners. Wrap ends with remaining pipe cleaner. Use bobby pins to secure bottom braid and shape into letter C.

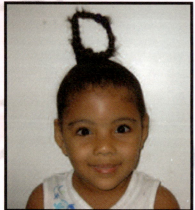

D - Make 1 ponytail on your top right side of your crown slightly off centre. Divide hair into 2 braids with 2 pipe cleaners for each braid. Wrap ends with remaining pipe cleaner. Use bobby pins to secure bottom braid and shape into letter D.

Letters of the Alphabet

E - Make 1 ponytail on your top right side of your crown slightly off centre. Divide hair with 1 short braid for bottom letter and 1 long braid with 3 pipe cleaners. Halfway up, tie elastic, make one braid and 1 pipe cleaner for mid-section of E and finish off braid with the 2 pipe cleaners left. Secure bottom braid with bobby pin and shape into letter E.

F - Make 1 ponytail on your top right side of your crown slightly off centre. Braid with 3 pipe cleaners and halfway up use an elastic. Divide into two braids with one braid for mid-section of F. Finish off braid with the 2 pipe cleaners left and wrap ends and shape into letter F.

G - Make 1 ponytail on your top right side of your crown slightly off centre. Divide hair with 1 short braid with 1 pipe cleaner for bottom and 1 long braid with 2 pipe cleaners. Wrap ends with remaining pipe cleaner. Use bobby pins to secure bottom braid and shape into letter G.

Letters of the Alphabet

H - Section hair down the middle (centre) and make 2 ponytails at each side of top of crown. Use 3 pipe cleaners and 2 thick elastics for each braid. Halfway through the braid, divide a strand and braid it, then connect to other side. Now divide the remaining hair into 3 strands and finish braid. Slide long wooden stick along the back and into the elastic to secure and shape into letter H.

I - Make a ponytail at the top centre of your crown. Use 3 pipe cleaners and 2 thick elastics and begin to braid. At the end, you can use beads to the pipe cleaner and decorate it. Slide popsicle stick from the top of braid down to the elastic for support and shape into letter I.

J - Make 1 ponytail on your top left side of your crown slightly off centre. Divide hair with 1 short braid for bottom letter with 1 pipe cleaner and 1 long braid with 2 pipe cleaners. 3/4 way up use elastic and divide hair to make 2 braids. Wrap ends with remaining pipe cleaner and secure bottom braid with bobby pin and shape into letter J.

Letters of the Alphabet

K - Make 1 ponytail on top centre of your head. Use 3 pipe cleaners and begin to braid. Halfway up use elastic and separate the strands to make 3 braids. Wrap ends with remaining pipe cleaner and shape into letter K.

L - Make 1 ponytail on your top right side of your crown slightly off centre. Divide hair with 1 short braid for bottom letter and 1 long braid with 2 pipe cleaners. Wrap ends with remaining pipe cleaner and secure bottom braid with bobby pin and shape into letter L.

M - Section hair down the middle (centre) and make 2 ponytails at each side of top of crown. Use 3 pipe cleaners for each braid. Wrap hair ends with elastic and remaining pipe cleaner to connect the two braids and shape into letter M.

Letters of the Alphabet

N - Section hair down the middle (centre) and make 2 ponytails at each side of top of crown. Use 3 pipe cleaners for each braid. Your left side of the braid, leave some hair out for the middle part of the letter. Wrap hair ends with elastic and remaining pipe cleaner. Use a pipe cleaner to wrap the hair around and connect it to the top of the other braid and shape into letter N.

O - Make 1 ponytail at top centre of crown. Divide ponytail in half and make 2 braids with 2 black pipe cleaners for each braid. Wrap hair ends with pipe cleaner and join ends together. Use bobby pins to secure bottom braid and shape into letter O.

P - Make 1 ponytail on your top right side of your crown slightly off centre. Use 3 pipe cleaners and braid. Halfway up secure with elastic and make 2 braids. Wrap ends with remaining pipe cleaner and connect the braids and shape into letter P.

Letters of the Alphabet

Q - Make 1 ponytail at top centre of crown. Divide ponytail in half and make 2 braids with 2 black pipe cleaners for each braid. Wrap hair ends with pipe cleaner and join together. Use small piece of pipe cleaner and slide through bottom to finish letter Q. Use bobby pins to secure bottom braid and shape into letter Q.

R - Section hair down the middle and make 2 ponytails at each side of top of crown. Use 3 pipe cleaners and 2 thick elastics for each braid. When the braids are completed, start shaping your letter R and use bobby pins to secure and pipe cleaner to connect the ends. Slide wooden stick from the top to the end of elastic for support.

S - Make 1 ponytail slightly off top centre of the crown to your left. Divide hair into 2 braids, 1 short braid with 1 pipe cleaner for bottom of letter and long with 3 pipe cleaner for the top. Wrap hair ends with remaining pipe cleaner. Use bobby pins to secure bottom braid and shape into letter S.

Letters of the Alphabet

T - Make one ponytail at top centre of crown. Use 3 pipe cleaners into the elastic and begin to braid. About 3/4 ways secure with elastic and divide hair into 2 braids and wrap hair ends with remaining pipe cleaner and shape into letter T.

U - Make one ponytail at top centre of crown. Divide hair into 2 braids with 3 pipe cleaners for each braid. Wrap hair ends with remaining pipe cleaner and use bobby pins to pin bottom of letter and shape into letter U.

V - Make one ponytail at top centre of crown. Divide hair into 2 braids with 3 pipe cleaners for each braid. Wrap hair ends with remaining pipe cleaner and shape into letter V.

Letters of the Alphabet

W - Section hair in the middle to make 2 ponytails, and with one of the ponytails, leave some hair out to form the middle part of the letter. Use 3 pipe cleaners for each braid and wrap hair ends with remaining pipe cleaner. For the middle part use a pipe cleaner and wrap the hair around to join it to the bottom of the braid and shape into letter W.

X - Section hair in the middle and make 2 ponytails at top of crown. Use 3 pipe cleaners into elastic for each braid. Wrap ends with remaining pipe cleaner and crisscross the braids with hair pin and shape into letter X.

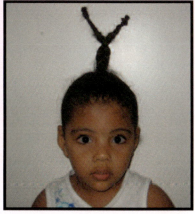

Y - Make one ponytail at centre top of crown, add 3 pipe cleaners into elastic and start braiding. Halfway up the braid, secure with an elastic and divide hair into 2 braids. Wrap ends with remaining pipe cleaner and shape into letter Y.

Letters of the Alphabet

Z - Make one ponytail at centre top of crown. Divide hair into 2 braids; 1 short for bottom of letter using 1 pipe cleaner and long for top of letter using 3 pipe cleaners. Wrap ends with remaining pipe cleaner and small elastic. Use bobby pins to secure bottom braid and shape into letter Z.

CPSIA information can be obtained
at www.ICGtesting.com
Printed in the USA
LVIW011717121012
302420LV00002B